C000096343

1 MONTH OF
FREE
READING

at
www.ForgottenBooks.com

By purchasing this book you are eligible for one month membership to ForgottenBooks.com, giving you unlimited access to our entire collection of over 1,000,000 titles via our web site and mobile apps.

To claim your free month visit:
www.forgottenbooks.com/free1113260

ISBN 978-0-331-37106-2
PIBN 11113260

This book is a reproduction of an important historical work. Forgotten Books uses
state-of-the-art technology to digitally reconstruct the work, preserving the original format
whilst repairing imperfections present in the aged copy. In rare cases, an imperfection in
the original, such as a blemish or missing page, may be replicated in our edition. We do,
however, repair the vast majority of imperfections successfully; any imperfections that
remain are intentionally left to preserve the state of such historical works.

Historic, archived document

Do not assume content reflects current
scientific knowledge, policies, or practices.

FOR RELEASE MONDAY, APRIL 20, 1959

(Continued on following page)

UNITED STATES DEPARTMENT OF AGRICULTURE
FOREIGN AGRICULTURAL SERVICE
WASHINGTON 25, D. C.

CONTENTS (Continued)   Page

ooOoo

PHILIPPINE COPRA, COCONUT OIL EXPORTS
DOWN ONE-THIRD IN FIRST QUARTER OF YEAR

        Philippine copra and coconut oil exports in the first 3 months of
the year were 87,831 long tons, oil basis. This represents a decline
of one-third from exports in the first quarter of 1958.

        Copra exports in January-March were less than two-thirds the volume
shipped in the first 3 months of 1958. Coconut oil shipments for the
same period were down one-fifth. Exports of desiccated coconut in January-
March were 7,803 short tons, against 11,838 tons in the comparable period
last year.

        The Philippine copra export price in mid-April was about $265 per
short ton c.i.f. Pacific Coast (mid-March--$257, mid-February--$255).
Local buying prices were reported at 53.50 to 54.50 pesos per 100
kilograms ($271.79 to $276.87 per long ton) resecada Manila, and 47 to
53 pesos ($238.77 to $269.25) in producing areas.

        See page 23 for tabulation of exports by country of destination.

IRISH FRUIT IMPORTERS AGAIN
PROTEST SPECIAL IMPORT LEVIES

Irish fruit importers have again protested the import duties on
canned fruit and juices and fresh citrus fruit. On canned fruits
such as apricots, pears, peaches and pineapple there is a special
levy of 4.4 cents per pound, plus the standard duty of 2.8 cents
per pound.

The trade has told the government that these substantial levies
have reduced sales of the affected commodities by substantially increasing prices to the consumer. It was conceded that the standard
duty of 2.8 cents per pound, in effect for many years is reasonable.
The trade maintains, however, that the retention of the special levy
is unjustified. It maintains that any duty which increases the over-
all price of an article by one-thirds to two-thirds is unfair.

A special levy of 60 percent ad valorem on prepared juices was
also protested as extremely excessive. Industry representatives
said it placed these juices "out of reach of the average consumer".
Similarly, the trade requested removal of a special 37½ percent ad
valorem on fresh lemons and grapefruit. There was a substantial
increase in orange sales following recent removal of this special
levy from that fruit.

MINIMUM EXPORT PRICES ANNOUNCED
FOR SPANISH SUMMER ORANGES

Minimum export prices for Valencia and Verna oranges have been
announced by the Spanish government. The minimums for these varieties
exported on consignment are set at $2.14 per standard box, averaging
66 pounds, and $3.21 for firm sales.

HIGHER PRICES CUT IRISH
CIGARETTE CONSUMPTION

Retail prices for tobacco products in Ireland have increased
greatly during the past 5 years, and the rise has reduced consumption. Cigarette production in Ireland in 1958 totaled 11.2 million
pounds, compared with 12.1 million in 1957, and 13.1 million in 1953.

In 1953, average retail prices for popular brands of cigarettes
were equivalent to U.S. 26 cents per pack of 20; the current average
price is around 43 cents--a rise of 66 percent. Other tobacco products also are higher than in 1953, but have not risen as much as
cigarette prices. These retail price increases have followed sharp
rises in duty rates.

AMERICAN-TYPE CIGARETTES
SELL FASTER IN EGYPT

American-blended type cigarettes continue to gain consumer acceptance in Egypt. Last year, this type of cigarette accounted for about 51 percent of Egypt's manufacture of all tobacco products, compared with 42 percent in 1957, and 36 percent in 1956. Although much of the leaf tobacco in these cigarettes is of U.S. origin, increasing quantities of substitutable leaf from other sources are being used.

The gain in output of American-type cigarettes has displaced the straight-oriental type to a considerable extent. In 1953, output of straight oriental brands exceeded production of the American-type. In 1958, however, the latter were nearly 5 times as important as oriental.

TOBACCO PRODUCTS: Egypt, approximate percentage output
of various products, 1954-58

Product	1954	1955	1956	1957	1958
	Percent	Percent	Percent	Percent	Percent
Cigarettes:					
American-blended.......:	29.7	32.0	35.8	42.0	51.2
Oriental...............:	27.4	25.2	22.1	18.2	11.8
Straight Virginia......:	13.0	13.0	13.2	12.2	8.3
Other:					
Roll-your-own					
(oriental)...........:	14.8	15.4	15.2	15.6	16.1
Pipe tobacco and					
small cigars.........:	13.9	13.3	12.7	11.2	11.6
Chewing tobacco........:	1.2	1.1	1.0	0.8	1.0
Total.............:	100.0	100.0	100.0	100.0	100.0

PORTUGAL INCREASES PRICES
FOR TOBACCO PRODUCTS

On March 10, 1959, the Portuguese Ministry of Finance authorized the 2 local manufacturing firms to increase prices of tobacco products about 6 percent. Although this will benefit manufacturers, the latter state that the cost-price squeeze they have faced for the past several years, due to rising leaf costs and controlled prices, will remain almost as serious as in the past.

U.S. TOBACCO EXPORTS
DROP IN FEBRUARY

   U.S. exports of unmanufactured tobacco in February 1959 totaled 17.0
million pounds--a drop of 26 percent from February a year ago. The value
of February 1959 exports also was lower than in February 1958--$12.0 mil-
lion compared with $16.6 million.

   Exports of flue-cured, Burley, dark-fired Kentucky-Tennessee, and
Green River were well below those for February 1958. There were gains
for Virginia fire-cured, Maryland, cigar wrapper, and cigar binder.

   For the first 2 months of 1959, exports totaled 44.5 million pounds--
down about 5 percent from the 47 million shipped out in January-February
1958. On a fiscal year basis, exports continue to hold up well in com-
parison with a year ago. For the period July 1958-February 1959, exports
totaled 365.2 million pounds, valued at $271.9 million compared with
358.2 million pounds, valued at $262.9 million, for the first 8 months of
the 1957-58 fiscal year.

   TOBACCO, UNMANUFACTURED: U.S. exports, by type and export weight,
   February and January-February 1958 and 1959, with percent change

Type	February		:Percent :change	Jan.-Feb.		:Percent :change
	1958	1959		1958	1959	
	:1,000 :pounds	:1,000 :pounds	:Percent	:1,000 :pounds	:1,000 :pounds	:Percent
Flue-cured..............	:15,664	:11,008	: -29.7	:33,604	:32,447	: -3.4
Burley..................	: 3,154	: 1,837	: -41.8	: 5,389	: 3,349	: -37.9
Dark-fired Ky.-Tenn. ...:	1,941	: 1,252	: -35.5	: 2,932	: 3,415	: +16.5
Va. fire-cured 1/.......:	176	: 665	:+277.8	: 641	: 1,296	:+102.2
Maryland................:	498	: 829	: +66.5	: 1,469	: 1,325	: -9.8
Green River.............:	198	: 55	: -72.2	: 209	: 167	: -20.1
One Sucker..............:	212	: 5	: ---	: 220	: 175	: -20.5
Black Fat, etc. ....:	332	: 346	: +4.2	: 678	: 737	: +8.7
Cigar wrapper...........:	479	: 595	: +24.2	: 724	: 781	: +7.9
Cigar binder............:	78	: 253	:+224.4	: 547	: 391	: -28.5
Cigar filler............:	7	: 2	: ---	: 8	: 16	:+100.0
Other...................:	357	: 172	: -51.8	: 553	: 389	: -29.7
Total...............:	:23,096	:17,019	: -26.3	:46,974	:44,488	: -5.3
Declared value (million dollars).....:	16.6	: 12.0	: -27.7	: 34.5	: 32.1	: -7.0

1/ Includes sun-cured.

Compiled from records of the Bureau of the Census.

U. S. exports of tobacco products in February 1959 were valued at
$6.8 million.-up 11.5 percent from February a year ago. Exports of ciga-
rettes at 1,428 million pieces were up 14 percent, and chewing and snuff
showed an increase of 31 percent. Bulk smoking tobacco, and cigars and
cheroots were down about one-third from February 1958.

TOBACCO PRODUCTS: U.S. exports, February and January-February
1958 and 1959, with percent change

Products and value	February		Percent change	Jan.-Feb.		Percent change
	1958	1959		1958	1959	
Cigars and cheroots (1,000 pieces)	1,487	977	-34.3	1,779	1,559	-12.4
Cigarettes (million pieces)	1,256	1,428	+13.7	2,598	2,778	+6.9
Chewing and snuff (1,000 pounds)	136	178	+30.9	274	247	-9.9
Smoking tobacco in pkgs. (1,000 pounds)	54	57	+5.6	101	105	+4.0
Smoking tobacco in bulk (1,000 pounds)	657	443	-32.6	1,214	883	-27.3
Total declared value (million dollars)	6.1	6.8	+11.5	12.4	13.1	+5.6

Compiled from records of the Bureau of the Census.

NEW ZEALAND LAMB
SLAUGHTER DROPS

The current New Zealand lamb slaughter season is ending. Lamb slaughter has fallen off sharply. Production of lamb was down this season due
to a drop in the average carcass weight of lambs. Mutton production, however, was up. Exports of lamb from New Zealand to the United States have
been dropping in recent months and through 1959 are expected to remain
slightly lower than a year earlier.

The main beef slaughtering season is now commencing in New Zealand,
but industry spokesmen say killings are likely to be lower than last year.
Although large quantities of boneless beef are still being shipped to the
United States, this season's total is expected to be below last year. Due
to sharp increases in the price of beef in the United Kingdom, New Zealand's
shipments to that market are expected to increase over last year, when most
of its beef exports went to the United States.

U.K. BEEF PRICES HIGH

Prices received by farmers on the open market for beef cattle in the United Kingdom rose sharply last year and have remained high so far during 1959. The average price of Grade I steers on English-Welsh markets during the week ended April 1 reached 175 shillings per English hundredweight ($21.88 per hundred pounds). This is 23 percent above the same week in 1958.

Reduced imports of beef from Argentina and a slackening of domestic beef production have not been offset by increased imports from Australia and New Zealand. Hog, sheep, and lamb prices have remained substantially level in spite of increased production.

Higher U.K. prices for beef will probably cause such exporting countries as Australia and New Zealand either to shift some of their exports from the United States to the United Kingdom or at least to reduce the rate of increase in shipments to the United States.

SUBSIDIZE FREIGHT RATES ON
SPANISH CITRUS FOR NORWAY

The "S-SEKRETARIAT" an organization in Norway which serves the interest of the Spanish trade with Norway has announced a private freight subsidy system to encourage Norwegian imports of Spanish summer citrus. Subsidies of $0.56 cents per box for shipments around March 23 and $0.70 cents per box for early April shipments of Verna and Valencia varieties will be paid. The present freight rate before subsidy from Spain to Norway is $1.02.

A private fund collected from firms exporting goods to Spain will be used to finance the subsidy. These subsidies have been announced only for shipments through early April, while the first arrival of California citrus is scheduled for early May. However, fruit trade representatives expect the subsidy to be extended and made effective for shipments arriving in competition with this U. S. fruit.

Present quotations for early April delivery of Spanish Vernas, after deducting subsidy, is about $6.65 per box compared to $7.70 for California Valencias, both c.i.f.

U. S. LARD EXPORTS RISE
IN JANUARY-FEBRUARY

U. S. lard exports during the first 2 months of 1959 were 99 million pounds, up sharply from the 70 million shipped during the comparable months of 1958.

Shipments to Cuba rose sharply. In large part the increase in Cuban imports represents a return to normal marketings which were disrupted in late 1958. The United Kingdom also increased its imports from the United States as the price of U. S. lard became more competitive with that of European producers.

TALLOW PRODUCTION AND
IMPORTS UP IN YUGOSLAVIA

Tallow production in Yugoslavia in 1958 was 18 million pounds, up
about 5 percent from 1957.

Imports account for a large part of total supply. In recent years,
all tallow has been imported from the United States. U.S. exports to
Yugoslavia were up moderately in 1958.

Soap production, however, declined slightly and the use of detergents
is increasing. Present output of soap is about two-thirds of factory
capacity. Government plans call for increasing soap production until the
industry is operating at its full capacity.

COLOMBIA RELAXES BANS ON
BREEDING CATTLE IMPORTS

The Colombian Ministry of Agriculture has announced the easing of
restrictions on imports of breeding cattle from countries with foot-and-
mouth disease. This is a significant step toward stimulating imports of
cattle to improve Colombian dairy and beef breeds.

The Ministry has emphasized the necessity of obtaining carefully
selected animals and pointed out that the new quarantine and sanitary gegu-
lations allow the importation of animals from areas affected by types of
foot-and-mouth disease not found in Colombia.

ARGENTINA, NEW ZEALAND CHIEF SOURCES
OF U. S. RED MEAT IMPORTS

The 2 leading exporters of red meats to the United States in 1958
were Argentina and New Zealand. Of the 828-million-pound import total,
Argentina supplied 26 percent (217 million pounds) and New Zealand, 23
percent (191 million pounds). Other leading suppliers were Canada, 14
percent, and Mexico, 9 percent.

The principal items in the total imports were boneless beef, 34 percent; processed pork, 16 percent; processed beef, 14 percent; and miscellaneous processed meats, 17 percent.

New Zealand was the leading supplier of boneless beef, with 53 percent of the total. Mexico was second with 24 percent.

Among the exporters of processed pork to the United States the
Netherlands led with 32 percent. Denmark and Poland followed closely
with 29 and 21 percent, respectively.

Argentina supplied 88 percent of the miscellaneous processed meats
and 75 percent of the processed beef products.

	Million pounds	Million pounds	Million pounds	Million pounds	Million pounds	Million pounds	Million pounds	Million pounds	Million pounds	Million pounds
Argentina..........	--	2	89	--	--	--	--	--	2/ 125	217
New Zealand........	20	152	--	10	--	--	5	--	2	191
Canada.............	29	21	--	3	51	11	1	--	4/ 3/	116
Mexico.............	6	67	--	--	--	--	1	1	--	75
Netherlands........	--	--	--	--	--	42	--	--	--	42
Denmark............	--	--	--	--	--	38	--	3	--	41
Australia..........	--	16	--	--	--	--	--	14	--	30
Poland.............	--	--	--	--	--	27	--	--	--	27
Ireland............	--	23	--	--	--	--	--	--	--	23
Paraguay...........	--	--	9	--	--	--	--	6	--	15
Brazil.............	--	--	10	--	--	--	--	3	--	13
Uruguay............	--	--	10	--	--	--	--	--	--	10
Germany, West......	--	--	--	--	--	7	--	--	--	7
Dominican Republic	2	2	--	--	--	--	--	--	--	4
Costa Rica.........	1	--	--	--	--	--	--	--	--	3
Italy..............	--	--	--	--	--	1	--	1	3/	1
Iceland............	--	--	--	--	--	--	1	--	4/ 2	1
Other countries...	1	--	1	1	--	5	2	2	--	12
Total........	59	281	119	14	51	131	7	17	142	828
Percentage of total meat imports	Percent	Percent	Percent	Percent	Percent	Percent	Percent	Percent	Percent	Percent
	7	34	14	2	6	16	1	2	17	5/ 100

1/ Only types imported are tabulated; imports of less than 500,000 pounds not shown. 2/ Mainly boneless, lightly salted beef or mutton. 3/ Includes about 1 million pounds of other fresh or frozen meats. 4/ Includes about 1 million pounds of variety meats. 5/ Approximately 1 percent of total imports consisted of variety meats and other fresh or frozen meats.

UBA SELLS CATTLE
O HONDURAS

The Agricultural and Industrial Bank of Cuba and the National
)evelopment Bank of Honduras have entered into an agreement whereby they
rill jointly finance purchases of Cuban cattle by Honduran cattlemen.

The first transaction will involve 300 head of breeding cattle,
iostly Brahman and Brown Swiss. Prospects are good for substantially
;reater sales.

IRAZILIAN BEEF TO SWITZERLAND
;Y AIR FREIGHT

Frigorifico Anglo S. A. in Rio de Janeiro recently received an order
'rom a customer in Basel, Switzerland, for 55 tons of filet mignon steaks.
'he Brazilian firm is shipping 2 tons weekly by air.

IEW ZEALAND SELLS BREEDING CATTLE
.ND SHEEP TO KENYA AND PHILIPPINES

New Zealand recently shipped 1,000 head of Shorthorn breeding cattle
,o the Philippines and 1,300 head of sheep to Kenya. The shipment of
;heep, which included Corriedale, Romney, Southdown, and Hampshiredown
)reeds, was valued at $50,000 to $55,000.

IO SURPLUS BEEF IN SOUTH AFRICA

In reply to British inquiries about buying South African beef, the
;eneral manager of the South African Meat Board has stated that there is
io surplus of beef in South Africa at present and none is likely in the
'oreseeable future.

:TALY LIMITS BEEF IMPORTS

Italy has banned imports of all fresh, chilled, or frozen beef except
'rozen manufacturing beef for processing. This is in response to heavy
)ressure by agricultural organizations to protect domestic producers (see
'oreign Crops and Markets, October 6, 1958).

Beef imports will be limited whenever the price of live cattle at
;elected Italian markets is less than 30,500 lire per metric quintal
[220.46 pounds)--$22.14 per 100 pounds. When the price of cattle is above
;his limit, all types of beef may be imported. The price of first-grade
;teers at Milan fell from an average of 35,429 lire per quintal in 1957 to
33,685 in 1958. The price had fallen further to 30,500 lire by the end of
March 1959.

Italy has become an important importer of beef during the past few
years. During 1958 it took about 260 million pounds of beef, mostly from
Argentina and Denmark.

SPAIN HAD RECORD DRIED FIG
PACK; EXPORTS UP SHARPLY

Due to exceptionally favorable weather, Spain had a "bumper" pack of
dried figs in 1958. Production is currently estimated at 33,000 short
tons, compared with 24,000 tons in 1957 and 19,800 tons in 1956.

Spanish dried fig exports of about 4,100 short tons in calendar year
1958 were strikingly larger than in recent years:

1954 -	1,388 short tons	1956 -	434 short tons
1955 -	948 " "	1957 -	962 " "
	1958 - 4,130 short tons		

The remarkable increase in exports is due to three factors: larger
production, favorable export prices, and stricter standards. In the past,
Spain's biggest handicap was its failure to deliver a standardized high-
quality product. However, recent export inspection and quality control
measures have stimulated export sales.

Spanish export figures do not include shipments of fig paste, for
which data are unobtainable.

Minimum export prices established last fall (converted at the official rate of 42 pesetas per U.S. dollar) were as follows:

Dried figs, in 10 kilogram bags--7.0 cents per pound
   "   "   " 10   "   boxes--8.2 "   "   "
Edible fig paste, in 50 kilogram boxes--7.0 cents per pound
Inedible fig paste, in 50 kilogram boxes--6.2 cents per pound

Minimum export prices were also set for dried figs in various con-
sumer-size packages. Prices to growers for the 1958 crop ranged from 5.4
cents to 8.0 cents per pound at the official rate.

Norway and France, combined, took 91 percent of 1958 Spanish dried
fig exports; 2,008 tons went to Norway and 1,737 tons to France. Both
countries are relatively new fig customers for Spain; in 1957 France
purchased none and Norway only 198 tons from Spain.

FIGS, DRIED: Spain, estimated exports by countries of
destination, calendar 1958

Destination	Short tons	Destination	Short tons
Brazil......................:	213	:Germany, West........:	46
Cuba........................:	54	:Norway................:	2,008
France......................:	1,737	:Other.................:	72
		Total...........:	4,130

AUSTRALIA PLANTING
MORE ALMONDS

Australia's 1958 commercial almond harvest amounted to 1,088 short tons, in-shell basis--enough to satisfy 60 percent of the country's nee(Though still relatively small, the Australian almond industry is slowly developing as new trees come into bearing.

The Commonwealth Bureau of Census and Statistics lists the followi] tree numbers, and tonnages harvested, for the past 6 seasons:

| Year | Number of trees | | | Productio] |
	Bearing	Non-bearing	Total	
	1,000 trees	1,000 trees	1,000 trees	Short tons
1953...................:	333	76	409	1,088
1954...................:	338	62	400	955
1955...................:	363	62	425	804
1956...................:	377	73	450	1,106
1957...................:	361	78	439	948
1958...................:	373	86	459	1,088

Between 85 and 90 percent of Australian almonds are grown in South Australia State. Of the several varieties of almonds grown--including IXL and Peerless--Hatche's Nonpareil is considered most promising.

Small quantities of Australian almonds are exported, chiefly to Co] wealth countries. Italy is the principal country shipping almonds to Australia.

U.S. RICE EXPORTS DOWN IN FEBRUARY

February exports of U.S. rice (in terms of milled) at 596,000 bags (100 pounds) were less than the 808,000 bags exported in January, and sharply below the 1,109,000 bags shipped in February a year earlier. C and European countries continued to be the main destinations.

An outstanding feature of the February shipments was the fact that only rice moving under Title I of Public Law 480 sales for foreign currencies was 22,000 bags to Pakistan. All other shipments except those moving under bater arrangements to the United Kingdom and West Germany were for cash. Commercial sales were therefore higher in February this year despite the drop in total shipments.

Rice exports in the first 7 months of the current marketing year (August-February) were approximately 6,700,000 bags--around 300,000 bag less than in the first 7 months of the preceding year. Cuba and the Philippines took 39 and 17 percent, respectively, of the exports. Sixt percent went to Europe, principally to West Germany, the United Kingdom Belgium-Luxembourg, and the Netherlands.

RICE: United States exports, in terms of milled, to specified countries,
        February 1959, with comparisons 1/

Country of destination	August- July 1957-58	August-February 1957-58	August-February 1958-59 2/	February 1958	February 1959 2/
	1,000 cwt.	1,000 cwt.	1,000 cwt.	1,000 cwt.	1,000 cwt.
Western Hemisphere:					
Canada ....:	293	213	202	14	15
British Honduras ....:	24	6	1	6	0
British West Indies ......:	103	97	16	2	3
Cuba ....:	4,246	2,688	2,627	377	280
Guatemala ....:	68	27	11	3	3/
Netherlands Antilles .....:	54	31	34	8	6
Nicaragua ....:	5	0	44	0	0
Bolivia ....:	44	22	0	0	0
Peru ....:	980	1	2	3/	3/
Other countries ....:	78	27	54	2	27
Total ....:	5,895	3,112	2,991	412	331
Europe:					
Belgium-Luxembourg ....:	76	52	173	8	49
West Germany ....:	30	0	435	0	46
Greece ....:	23	11	35	4	8
Netherlands ....:	14	3	131	0	22
Sweden ....:	12	8	26	3/	1
Switzerland ....:	32	30	23	0	4
United Kingdom ....:	34	3/	207	0	34
Other countries ....:	6	1	19	1	3
Total ....:	227	105	1,049	13	167
Asia:					
Ceylon ....:	331	0	550		
Indonesia ....:	753	0	89		
Korea, Republic of ....:	242	242	0	0	
Pakistan ....:	3,453	2,005	22	646	0
Philippine Republic ......:	554	377	1,140	3/	20
Saudi Arabia ....:	151	86	52	3/	6
Other Arabian States .....:	126	107	95	2	15
Other countries ....:	14	7	40	1	1
Total ....:	5,624	2,824	1,988	647	44
Total Oceania ....:	52	31	35	3	7
French Somaliland ....:	6	0	46	0	0
Liberia ....:	270	197	170	30	1
Other Africa ....:	17	9	29	2	3
Destination not specified ..:	17	11	11	1	1
Total exports (Census) :	12,108	6,289	6,319	1,108	554
Ryukyu Islands 4/ ....:	145	145	0	0	0
Section 416 donations ......:	683	572	380	1	42
World total ....:	12,936	7,006	6,699	1,109	596

1/ Includes brown, broken, screenings and brewers' rice and rough rice
converted to terms of milled at 65 percent. 2/ Preliminary. 3/ Less than
500 cwt. 4/ Programed by International Cooperation Administration and
shipped by the Army.

Source: Bureau of the Census and Department of Agriculture.

SHARP INCREASE IN YUGOSLAV
MILK OUTPUT

Milk production in Yugoslavia during 1958 increased 4 percent from 1957 to
set a new record of 5.5 billion pounds. The rise in cow's milk output, which
constitutes over 90 percent of total milk production, was attributed to higher
yield per cow.

Yugoslavia is stressing milk production and has a set a goal of 6.5 billion
pounds for 1961. Plans to improve milk supplies--especially of pasteurized milk-
include the building of new plants; importation of high-producing dairy cattle
from the Netherlands, Denmark, and Switzerland; and improvement of feeding
practices.

Private sale of milk in Belgrade was prohibited last year to eliminate the
sale of unpasteurized milk, either in the city's open markets or by home delivery
Milk is now largely purchased by general agricultural cooperatives located in
villages which operate milk collection stations. These cooperatives sell the mil
to the dairies. A regulation prohibiting the private sale of milk has been in
effect in Skoplje for several years.

Although milk supplies in the cities have improved, further efforts are
needed in order to organize efficient and sanitary production, collection, and
handling of milk. Dairy officials believe that the cost of the present system
tends to increase retail milk prices. They hope to bring about a reduction in
production costs and thus lower retail prices. This, along with an advertising
program, is expected to raise milk consumption.

CANADIAN WHEAT AND FLOUR EXPORTS DOWN

Canadian wheat and flour exports during July-February 1958-59 were down abou
4 million bushels from the corresponding months of 1957-58. The decrease was
almost entirely in wheat exports.

The United Kingdom, Japan, and West Germany continue to be the major markets
for Canadian wheat. Exports to these countries were slightly above those of a
year earlier. The most pronounced reduction was in exports to the Netherlands.
In addition to this drop of about 6 million bushels, no wheat went to the U.S.S.R.
and Poland, compared with 7.4 and 2.5 million bushels to these countries, respectively, in the corresponding months a year earlier.

Flour exports to the United Kingdom during July-February 1958-59 were a littl
larger than a year earlier. Exports to the Philippines and Venezuela, also
important flour markets, were somewhat below those in the first 8 months of 1957-5
These reductions were more than offset by these countries' increased wheat import
for use in newly established flour mills.

On the basis of Canada's 1958-59 marketing year (August-July) wheat and flou
exports during August-February were 162 million bushels, against 170 million
bushels during the first 7 months of 1957-58.

WHEAT AND FLOUR: Canadian exports by country of destination,
July-February 1957-58 and July-February 1958-59

Destination	July-February 1957-58			July-February 1958-59		
	Wheat	Flour 1/	Total	Wheat	Flour 1/	Total
	1,000 bushels:	1,000 bushels:	1,000 bushels:	1,000 bushels:	1,000 bushels:	1,000 bushels
Western Hemisphere:						
United States .....:	4,020:	1,092 :	5,112:	2,177:	1,097 :	3,274
British West Indies:	3:	3,372 :	3,375:	4:	3,290 :	3,294
Central America ...:	197:	921 :	1,118:	102:	1,229 :	1,331
Cuba ....:	1:	338 :	339:	1:	199 :	200
Ecuador ....:	212:	— :	212:	627:	— :	627
Peru ....:	1,259:	24 :	1,283:	794:	19 :	813
Venezuela ....:	138:	2,195 :	2,333:	1,746:	970 :	2,716
Others ....:	— :	1,133 :	1,133:	— :	1,251 :	1,251
Total ....:	5,830:	9,075 :	14,905:	5,451:	8,055 :	13,506
Europe:						
Austria ....:	2,000:	— :	2,000:	1,772:	— :	1,772
Belgium-Luxembourg :	7,407:	177 :	7,584:	8,208:	215 :	8,423
France ....:	754:	— :	754:	1,088:	— :	1,088
Germany, West .....:	19,071:	— :	19,071:	21,440:	— :	21,440
Ireland ....:	1,435:	1 :	1,436:	3,224:	— :	3,224
Italy ....:	545:	— :	545:	523:	1 :	524
Netherlands ....:	15,316:	1 :	15,317:	9,439:	6 :	9,445
Norway ....:	2,346:	— :	2,346:	2,617:	— :	2,617
Poland ....:	2,497:	— :	2,497:	— :	— :	—
Switzerland ....:	3,259:	2/ :	3,259:	4,724:	— :	4,724
U.S.S.R. ....:	7,387:	— :	7,387:	— :	— :	—
United Kingdom ....:	62,387:	8,597 :	70,984:	62,673:	8,728 :	71,401
Others ....:	933:	109 :	1,042:	1,183:	92 :	1,275
Total ....:	125,337:	8,885 :	134,222:	116,891:	9,042 :	125,933
Asia:						
China ....:	— :	— :	— :	1,643:	— :	1,643
India ....:	10,309:	20 :	10,329:	6,665:	2 :	6,667
Israel ....:	— :	— :	— :	850:	— :	850
Japan ....:	25,259:	529 :	25,788:	25,454:	447 :	25,901
Pakistan ....:	1,236:	2/ :	1,236:	2,327:	— :	2,327
Philippine Republic:	— :	3,497 :	3,497:	766:	2,928 :	3,694
Others ....:	190:	1,127 :	1,317:	453:	2,551 :	3,004
Total ....:	36,994:	5,173 :	42,167:	38,158:	5,928 :	44,086
Africa ....:	407:	815 :	1,222:	3,093:	1,178 :	4,271
Oceania ....:	411:	29 :	440:	— :	10 :	10
Unspecified ....:	— :	— :	— :	366:	— :	366
World total ....:	168,979:	23,977 :	192,956:	163,959:	24,213 :	188,172

1/ Grain equivalent.   2/ Less than 500 bushels.

Beginning with this issue, the source of information is the Board of Grain
Commissioners for Canada.

FINLAND BARTERS BUTTER
FOR RUSSIAN WHEAT

Finland and the Soviet Union are exchanging 6,000 metric tons
(13,227,600 pounds) of Finnish butter for about 68,000 tons (2,498,500
bushels) of Russian wheat during the 6 months ending June 30, 1959,
under terms of the second half of a butter-for-wheat barter agreement
signed a year ago.

Under this agreement, the two countries traded slightly over
6,000 tons of butter and about 50,000 tons (1,837,150 bushels) of
wheat in the last 6 months of 1958. Finland is receiving a larger
amount of Russian wheat during the current 6-month period because of
expected higher world butter prices.

By the end of January 1959, Finland's wheat import commitments
under the first half of the agreement totaled 52,441 tons (1,926,800
bushels), of which 42,341 tons (1,555,700 bushels) had arrived in
Finland. The balance of 10,100 tons (371,000 bushels) was resold to
Switzerland, shipped direct from Russian Black Sea ports via Rotterdam
and the Rhine River.

Finland is permitted by the agreement to resell the Russian wheat
because of inadequate storage space. Resale of this wheat is also
necessitated by the provision in the butter-for-wheat barter agreement
that Finland's wheat imports under it shall not displace its bread-
grain import quotas specified in the annual Russo-Finnish bilateral
trade agreements. The bilateral agreement for 1959 was signed March
13, 1959 (see Foreign Crops and Markets, April 13).

Finland made the butter-for-wheat agreement primarily because of
restrictions against butter sales in the British market. These
restrictions were lifted in December 1958.

FREE WORLD HARVESTS
RECORD RICE CROP

The rice harvest in the countries of the Free World in 1958-59 is
the largest on record. Unusually favorable weather in a majority of
the countries is the principal factor. Also, rice acreage is 3.5
million acres over the previous record of 200.6 million acres in
1956-57.

Free World production of rough rice in 1958-59 (August-July) is
tentatively estimated at 296 billion pounds, compared with 266 billion
pounds in 1957-58 and the previous record of 286 billion in 1956-57.
The estimate is 17 percent above the average from 1950-51 through 1954-55.

The production gain of 3 percent over the previous record crop is
primarily in the principal importing countries of Asia. Total output
of the main exporters in 1958-59, though 17 percent above the poor
crop of the preceding year, approximates the 1956-57 level.

RICE (rough): Production in specified countries of the Free World,
average 1950-51/54-55, annual 1955-56 to 1958-59 (August-July) 1/

Country	Average 1950-51 to 1954-55	1955-56	1956-57	1957-58 2/	1958-59 2/
	Million pounds	Million pounds	Million pounds	Million pounds	Million pounds
Exporting countries:					
Argentina ....:	394.1	362.0	424.6	477.5	3/ 485.0
Australia ....:	170.3	198.5	178.9	237.5	240.0
Brazil ....:	7,182.5	7,691.4	9,151.2	3/8,900.0	3/9,200.0
British Guiana ....:	279.7	285.0	265.0	235.0	3/340.0
Burma ....:	13,900.0	14,400.0	15,700.0	13,000.0	17,900.0
Cambodia ....:	2,817.0	2,645.5	3,368.6	2,755.0	3,000.0
Egypt ....:	1,829.4	2,400.0	2,750.0	2,900.0	1,750.0
Italy ....:	1,881.5	1,939.4	1,461.1	1,316.1	1,600.0
South Vietnam .....:	5,200.0	6,210.0	6,635.0	6,285.0	7,700.0
Spain ....:	757.9	857.0	846.5	855.0	860.0
Taiwan ....:	4,565.0	5,266.4	5,279.3	5,356.5	5,400.0
Thailand ....:	15,281.2	16,167.7	18,291.6	12,562.2	16,100.0
Surinam ....:	126.4	142.3	156.9	121.2	195.0
United States .....:	5,002.6	5,590.2	4,945.9	4,293.5	4,701.5
Total ....:	59,387.6	64,155.4	69,454.6	59,294.5	69,471.5
Importing countries:					
Ceylon ....:	1,223.4	1,506.0	1,290.1	1,345.0	1,450.0
Cuba ....:	320.0	475.0	615.0	575.0	500.0
India ....:	82,150.0	91,211.3	95,112.4	83,688.3	100,200.0
Indonesia ....:	23,118.3	24,791.3	25,243.7	25,500.0	3/25,000.0
Japan ....:	26,316.6	33,958.9	29,862.4	31,430.4	32,884.8
Korea, South ......:	6,546.0	7,000.0	6,000.0	7,400.0	7,700.0
Malaya ....:	1,453.4	1,493.8	1,733.8	1,761.7	1,600.0
Pakistan ....:	28,023.9	24,230.4	30,280.5	28,541.8	29,400.0
Peru ....:	553.8	536.2	519.2	595.2	550.0
Philippine Republic :	6,603.3	7,216.2	7,376.3	7,038.9	7,500.0
Total ....:	176,308.7	192,419.1	198,033.4	187,876.3	206,784.8
Other countries .....:	17,032.9	17,675.2	18,605.7	19,108.0	19,500.0
Free World total :	252,729.2	274,249.7	286,093.7	266,278.8	295,800.0

1/ Crops harvested in Northern Hemisphere during the latter part of the year,
together with those harvested in Asia from November to May, are combined with
crops harvested in Southern Hemisphere countries during the first part of the
following year. 2/ Preliminary. 3/ Tentative and unofficial forecast.

Foreign Agricultural Service. Prepared or estimated on the basis of official
statistics of foreign governments, reports of United States officers, results
of office research and other information.

CLOVE OUTPUT DROPS
IN ZANZIBAR-PEMBA

Early estimates indicate a 1958-59 "off-year" clove harvest totaling
only 11 million pounds in Zanzibar and Pemba. The 1957-58 crop was a
record 54 million pounds.

U.S. GRASS AND LEGUME SEED EXPORTS
DOWN SHARPLY IN FEBRUARY

The normal seasonal downtrend reflected in U.S. exports of grass and
legume seeds in February was greatly accented by a sharp decline in shipments of alfalfa and "other" grass seeds.

The crop-year total from July through February is more than 6 million
pounds below last season's shipments for the same 8-month period. This
is largely due to the short-fall in exports of alfalfa and "other" grass
seeds which more than offset the gains in "other" clovers, fescue, Kentucky
bluegrass, and timothy. Canada, West Germany, the Netherlands, France,
and Japan received the largest shipments in February.

GRASS AND LEGUME SEEDS: U.S. exports, February 1959,
with comparisons

Kind of seed	February		July 1-February 28	
	1958	1959	1957-58	1958-59
	1,000 pounds	1,000 pounds	1,000 pounds	1,000 pounds
Alfalfa, certified.................	1,082	574	1/	1/
Alfalfa, uncertified...............	894	686	1/	1/
Alfalfa, total.....................	1,976	1,260	15,036	7,959
Alsike............................	168	0	504	387
Ladino............................	107	149	1/	1/
Clovers, other....................	171	426	2,973	4,407
Bentgrass.........................	467	367	1/	1/
Fescue............................	319	236	2,761	3,223
Kentucky bluegrass................	219	296	835	1,663
Orchard...........................	27	21	159	329
Redtop............................	227	47	602	378
Timothy...........................	343	469	1,946	2,339
Grasses, other...................	1,367	285	10,295	8,351
Total.....................	5,391	3,556	35,111	29,036

1/ Prior to January 1, 1958, certified and uncertified alfalfa combined;
Ladino included in "other clovers"; and bentgrass included in "other
grasses".

YUGOSLAVIA BUYS SOYBEANS
FROM COMMUNIST CHINA

Yugoslavia has contracted for 21,000 metric tons (771,600 bushels) of soybeans from Communist China for delivery during April-June of this year. Imports of soybeans in 1958 are estimated at around 10,000 tons (370,000 bushels), mostly from Red China; 1957 imports totaled 11,496 tons (422,400 bushels), all from Red China.

DOMINICAN REPUBLIC EXPORTS
MORE COFFEE IN 1958

Coffee exports from the Dominican Republic increased from 361,483 bags in 1957 to 429,200 bags in 1958; the United States was the leading buyer both years. Exports during 1959 are expected to drop considerably from last year's level.

U.S. COTTON IMPORTS
UP IN FEBRUARY

U.S. imports of cotton (for consumption) were equivalent to 1,636 bales of 500 pounds gross weight in February 1959, compared with 1,009 bales in January, and 2,276 bales in February 1958.

The February imports consisted largely of Tanguis cotton from Peru which entered under the Tanguis category of the modified 1958-59 long-staple global quota. The 3,125-bale portion of the quota set aside for Tanguis is now filled. Other categories of the 95,000-bale long-staple quota were filled shortly after the beginning of the current long-staple quota year on August 1, 1958.

Cotton imports during August-February 1958-59 totaled 125,000 bales, down slightly from 129,000 bales in the corresponding months of 1957-58. Principal sources of the August-February 1958-59 imports, with comparable 1957-58 figures in parentheses, were: Egypt 58,000 bales (30,000); Mexico 33,000 (73,000); and Peru 26,000 (14,000). Smaller quantities were imported from Pakistan, India, Sudan, Brazil, and Aden.

U.S. IMPORTS MORE COTTON LINTERS

U.S. imports of cotton linters, mostly felting qualities, were 17,000 bales (500 pounds gross) in February 1959, up 13 percent from the 15,000 bales imported in January 1959, and 21 percent above imports of 14,000 bales in February 1958. Imports during August-February 1958-59 totaled 106,000 bales, compared with 91,000 bales in the corresponding 1957-58 period.

Principal sources of linters imports during August-February 1958-59, with comparable 1957-58 figures in parentheses, were: Mexico 85,000 bales (69,000); U.S.S.R. 9,000 (9,000); El Salvador 5,000 (2,000); Nicaragua 4,000 (1,000); and Guatemala 2,000 (1,000).

URUGUAYAN VEGETABLE OIL EXPORTS
MAY INCREASE THIS YEAR

Uruguay's exports of vegetable oils in 1959 are expected to be substantially larger than the sharply reduced quantity shipped in 1958.

Exports of linseed oil are forecast at 27,500 short tons--one fourth above 1958, but slightly below the large volume of 1957. Although the 1958-59 flaxseed crop was slightly smaller than the 1957-58 crop--2.8 and 2.9 million bushels, respectively--sharply reduced exports in 1958 created sizable stocks of linseed oil, which accounts for the additional quantity available for export this year.

For the first time in recent years, sunflower seed oil will be available for export. The good 1958 sunflower seed crop resulted in carryout stock on December 31, 1958, of around 11,000 tons of oil. Originally, export quotas were issued for 6,600 tons of oil, but were recently increased to 11,000 tons.

Although the 1959 sunflower seed crop now being harvested will be somewhat below last year, it appears that it will supply domestic oil needs. Production of seed in 1959 is estimated at 102,200 tons against 144,100 tons in 1958.

VEGETABLE OILS: Uruguayan exports and imports, by kind,
1957 and 1958, and forecast 1959

Items	1957	1958 1/	1959 2/
	Short tons	Short tons	Short tons
Exports:			
Linseed oil.......................:	28,219	20,757	27,500
Sunflower seed oil................:	0	0	11,000
Total...........................:	28,219	20,757	38,500
Imports:			
Olive oil.........................:	372	83	110
Coconut oil.......................:	2,036	452	550
Castor oil........................:	113	179	150
Tung oil..........................:	53	36	40
Total...........................:	2,574	750	850

1/ Preliminary. 2/ Forecast.

Uruguay imports small quantities of vegetable oils each year, and 1959 imports probably will be around the 1958 level. Foreign exchange shortages reduced 1958 imports by 70 percent from 1957, with smaller coconut oil purchases accounting for much of the drop.

ARGENTINA'S 1958-59 COTTON
CROP DOWN SHARPLY

Argentina's 1958-59 cotton crop, now being harvested, is unofficially estimated at 550,000 bales (500 pounds gross). This is a decline of 30 percent from
last season's record crop of 785,000 bales and 8 percent below average production
of 597,000 bales in the past 5 crop years. Excessive rainfall from December until
early March accounted for the smaller crop this year.

An estimated 290,000 to 300,000 acres planted to cotton this season were
abandoned because of floods. Acreage reaching maturity amounted to approximately
1,550,000 acres, compared with 1,655,000 acres harvested last season, and the
average of 1,403,000 for the past 5 seasons.

Minimum prices to producers for the 1958-59 crop were increased by 50 percent
from those prevailing in 1957-58. Prices for the current crop range from an equivalent of 14.91 cents per pound for Grade A lint cotton to 9.50 cents for Grade F,
compared with 9.94 and 6.34 cents, respectively, in 1957-58, based on the exchange
rate of 68 pesos per U.S. dollar.

As a part of the government's "austerity" program instituted early in 1959,
the official exchange rate of 18 pesos per dollar and the free rate of exchange
were replaced on January 12 by a single free rate. Since then, the value of the
peso has fluctuated from about 65 to 70 to the dollar. On April 3 it was 68 per
dollar.

Weaker demand and lower prices in world import markets caused Argentine cotton
exports to fall below 1,000 bales in 1957-58, compared with 51,000 bales in 1956-57.
As a result of the low level of exports and the record-high production, cotton
stocks increased nearly 60 percent during the 1957-58 season. To stimulate lagging
export sales in August 1958, the Argentine Government abolished the 10-percent exchange retention on exports of cotton and cotton linters. And in November, the
"aforo" on cotton exports was discontinued. Under the "aforo" system, part of the
foreign exchange proceeds from exports was negotiable at the official exchange rate
and the balance at the free rate.

Cotton exports from Argentina during the first 7 months (August-February) of
the current season were 21,000 bales. Principal destinations were Belgium, Japan,
and West Germany.

Cotton consumption in Argentina for 1958-59 is tentatively estimated at 550,000
bales. This compares with 520,000 bales used in 1957-58 and 543,000 bales used in
1956-57. Consumption during August-February of 1958-59 amounted to 306,000 bales,
compared with 288,000 a year earlier.

Since Argentina grows only upland-type cotton, small quantities of extra-long
staple cotton are imported from Peru and Egypt. The adoption of the free exchange
rate, together with the 40-percent surcharge on imported cotton is expected to hold
imports to an absolute minimum in 1958-59. During August-January, only 1,000 bales
were imported, in contrast to about 5,000 a year earlier. Cotton stocks on March
1, 1959, were reported at about 400,000 bales, compared with 175,000 on March 1,
1958.

JAPANESE COTTON CONSUMPTION AND
IMPORTS CONTINUE DOWNTREND

Cotton imports into Japan during the current season have continued the downtrend that began in 1957-58. During the first half (August-January) of the current
season, 1,060,000 bales (500 pounds gross) were imported. This was a decline of 8
percent from imports of 1,151,000 bales a year earlier. Imports are likely to
decline even further this season in view of the continuing cutbacks in textile production and the tendency of mills to limit purchases until lower-priced U.S. cotton
becomes available on August 1, 1959.

Imports of U.S. cotton in August-January declined to 317,000 bales (30 percent
of total cotton imports) compared with 483,000 bales or 42 percent in the same
months of 1957-58. This 34-percent decline reflects the shift to lower-priced
cotton from other countries. Japanese purchases of U.S. cotton in recent months
have been mostly lower qualities. It appears likely that the $60-million Export-
Import Bank cotton credit to Japan will not be fully utilized this season. Japan
is now expected to ask for a smaller Export-Import Bank credit for next season,
beginning August 1, 1959.

Imports from Mexico, Egypt, and Brazil were also smaller than a year earlier,
but those from Pakistan, India, Kenya, and Central America were much larger. Imports from principal sources during August-January 1958-59, with comparable 1957-58
figures in parentheses, were: United States 317,000 bales (483,000); Mexico 249,00
(330,000); Pakistan 117,000 (82,000); India 94,000 (44,000); Kenya 57,000 (594);
El Salvador 39,000 (23,000); Egypt 23,000 (36,000); Brazil 22,000 (92,000);
Guatemala 16,000 (491); Nicaragua 13,000 (7,000); and Peru 10,000 (7,000).

Cotton consumption by mills during the first half of this season was 1,039,000
bales (preliminary)--14 percent below the August-January level last season. The
decline is attributed to continuing production cutbacks in an effort to bring textile supplies more in line with demand. Due to overproduction in the first half of
1957-58, heavy textile stocks accumulated. Mills have reduced these stocks somewhat by voluntarily curbing operations during the last half of 1957-58 and thus far
in 1958-59. Output of pure cotton yarn in January 1959, at 68 million pounds, was
down 9 percent from 75 million pounds in December, and 12 percent from January 1958
output of 77 million pounds. Yarn production during August-January of the current
season totaled 438 million pounds, compared with 524 million in the same period
last season.

Operable spindleage on January 31, 1959, stood at 9,019,172--down 1,600 from
December 1958. The ratio of operated to operable spindleage in January was 70
percent, about the same as in December. Midseason cotton stocks on January 31,
1959, were reported at 523,000 bales. Stocks on August 1, 1958, were 536,000
bales.

Prices for U.S. cotton, c.i.f. Japan, now average around $1\frac{1}{4}$ cents a pound less
than at the beginning of this season. Some foreign growths are as much as 6 cents
a pound below August levels. On March 23, U.S. Middling 1-inch cotton was quoted
at 30.44 cents a pound, c.i.f. Osaka, while Pakistani Middling 1-inch was 26.32
cents.

COPRA: Philippine Republic, exports by country of destination,
March and January-March 1958 and 1959

Country of destination	1958 1/		1959 1/	
	March	January-March	March	January-March
	Long tons	Long tons	Long tons	Long tons
North America:				
United States.........:	20,804	49,413	30,985	61,229
Pacific Coast.......:	(20,804)	(49,413)	(30,985)	(61,229)
Canada................:	---	1,800	---	---
Total..........:	20,804	51,213	30,985	61,229
South America:				
Colombia..............:	6,184	15,753	---	---
Venezuela............:	---	1,500	3,466	6,372
Total..........:	6,184	17,253	3,466	6,372
Europe:				
Denmark...............:	1,000	4,800	---	500
France................:	750	3,310	---	---
Germany, West.........:	1,500	15,965	4,500	12,830
Italy.................:	---	1,400	---	---
Netherlands...........:	11,100	55,793	1,500	29,254
Norway................:	---	500	---	500
Spain.................:	---	---	---	3,500
Sweden................:	---	500	---	500
Optional discharge 2/.:	9,800	26,577	---	379
Total..........:	24,150	108,845	6,000	47,463
Asia:				
Israel................:	3,020	3,020	---	---
Lebanon...............:	500	2,700	---	---
Syria.................:	---	---	---	1,500
Total..........:	3,520	5,720	---	1,500
Grand total....:	54,658	183,031	40,451	116,564

1/ Preliminary. 2/ West Germany, Netherlands, or Belgium.

Source: Philippine trade sources.

COCONUT OIL: Philippine Republic, exports by country of destination,
March and January-March 1958 and 1959

Country of destination	1958 1/		1959 1/	
	March	January-March	March	January-March
	Long tons	Long tons	Long tons	Long tons
North America:				
United States.........:	4,564	17,406	3,862	13,026
Atlantic Coast......:	(4,564)	(17,406)	(3,438)	(11,603)
Pacific Coast.......:	(---)	(---)	(424)	(1,423)
Cuba..................:	350	350	---	---
Total..........:	4,914	17,756	3,862	13,026
Europe:				
Netherlands...........:	---	---	573	1,370
Total..........:	---	---	573	1,370
Grand total....:	4,914	17,756	4,435	14,396

1/ Preliminary.

Source: Philippine trade sources.

INDIA ALLOWS FURTHER
COTTON IMPORTS

The Government of India recently approved additional cotton imports
equivalent to 35,000 Indian bales of 400 pounds gross (about 28,500 bales
of 500 pounds gross) from Egypt and Sudan. This quota, which allows the
importation of cotton stapling 1-3/16 inches and over, will be combined
with a 25,000-bale quota for Egyptian and Sudanese cotton released earlier
this season. Mills will import equal quantities of the two growths from
the combined quotas of 60,000 bales.

The contracting period for Egyptian cotton continued through March 31,
1959, with a shipment deadline of May 31. Sudanese cotton can be contracte
through April 30, 1959, with shipment through June 30.

Total cotton imports allowed thus far in the 1958-59 season are equiva
lent to 426,000 bales of 400 pounds gross weight. This includes 96,000
bales (about 78,000 bales of 500 pounds gross weight) of cotton from the
United States obtained under Public Law 480.

CPSIA information can be obtained
at www.ICGtesting.com
Printed in the USA
BVHW041323281218
536518BV00015B/71/P

9 780331 371106